The Usborne Book of ART ideas

Fiona Watt

Designed by Amanda Barlow and Non Figg

Illustrated by Amanda Barlow, Non Figg,
Jan McCafferty, Lucy Parris, Nicola Butler,
Kathy Ward, Christina Adami and Rachel Wells

Photographs by Howard Allman
Based on ideas by Gill Figg and Ray Gibson

Contents

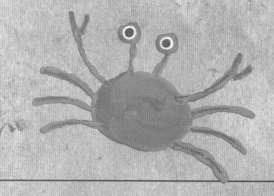

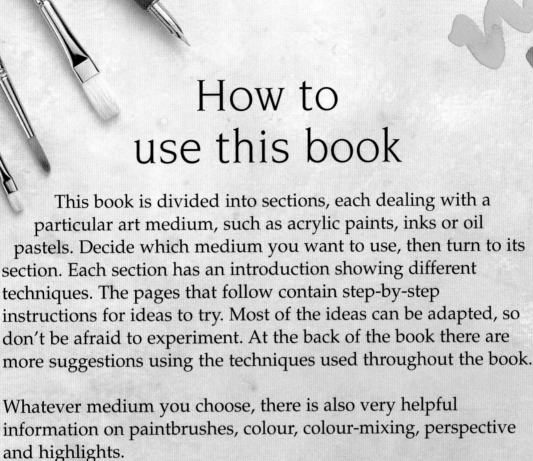

How to use this book

This book is divided into sections, each dealing with a particular art medium, such as acrylic paints, inks or oil pastels. Decide which medium you want to use, then turn to its section. Each section has an introduction showing different techniques. The pages that follow contain step-by-step instructions for ideas to try. Most of the ideas can be adapted, so don't be afraid to experiment. At the back of the book there are more suggestions using the techniques used throughout the book.

Whatever medium you choose, there is also very helpful information on paintbrushes, colour, colour-mixing, perspective and highlights.

Many of the pages in this book have painted backgrounds. These have been created using a variety of techniques. Find out on pages 84-85 how to make them.

Paper

The most suitable type of paper to use for each project is suggested under the main heading on each ideas page. Use this type if you have it - other paper may give you a different result. Look on page 4 for more information about paper.

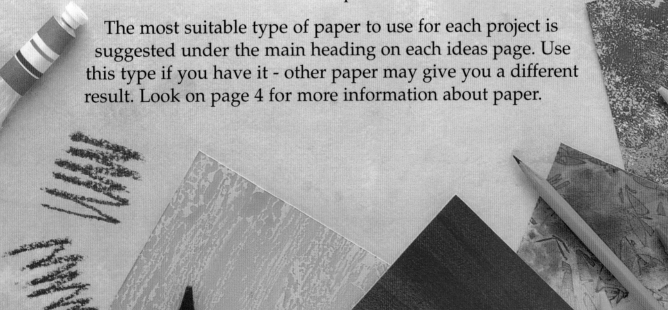

Art materials

The ideas in this book use materials which are easy to find in any shop that sells art equipment. These pages give you general information about art materials, but you'll find out more about them at the beginning of each section. Look on page 6 for information about brushes.

Paper

Under the heading on some pages, there is a suggestion of the type of paper to use. A few of the projects suggest cartridge or watercolour paper. You can buy this in books or in single sheets.

Cartridge paper is good for using with inks and pastels.

Typing or computer print-out paper.

Watercolour paper is special paper for watercolours.

Pastel paper or Ingres paper is special paper for pastels.

Tissue paper

Keep clean

Before you start, protect the surface you're working on with lots of newspaper. Put on an old shirt or apron to protect your clothes, too.

Paints

The type of paints used in this book are acrylic paint, watercolour paint, ready-mix and poster paint. They come in a variety of forms, such as dry blocks, tubes and bottles. See page 8 for some ideas of colours to buy.

The introduction to each section tells you how to mix that type of paint.

Acrylic paints come in tubes or bottles. Buy smallish tubes to begin with.

Watercolour blocks are more economical to use than tubes.

Ready-mix and poster paints are a bit like acrylics but are cheaper.

You can get gold and silver acrylic and poster paint.

Experiment with using different kinds of paper, such as brown wrapping paper.

Remember, if you use coloured paper, the colours you put on it will change.

Inks

Coloured inks come in small bottles. Use them with a brush or a dip pen for painting or drawing.

Inks come in lots of very bright colours.

You can get ink cartridges in lots of colours.

Pastels

There are ideas in this book which use chalk pastels and oil pastels. They are usually sold as a boxed set, but you can buy them individually.

Chalk pastels

Oil pastels give you much brighter colours than chalk pastels.

Wax crayons

Wax crayons usually come in sets. They aren't expensive and you can do some exciting things with them.

Pens

You will need a pen for some of the ideas in this book. You can also use an ordinary ink pen, cartridge pen or dip pen for drawing.

Felt-tip pen

Use a dip pen with ink in a bottle.

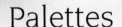

Cartridge pen

Other equipment

For some of the projects you may also need:- paper towels, old newspapers, a kitchen sponge, an old rag for wiping your brushes, yogurt pots and a large jam jar or plastic container for water.

Palettes

You will need something to mix your paints on. You don't need to have a proper mixing palette, use an old plate or a lid from a plastic container instead.

Use a white plate or lid. It will give you a good idea of the colour you are mixing.

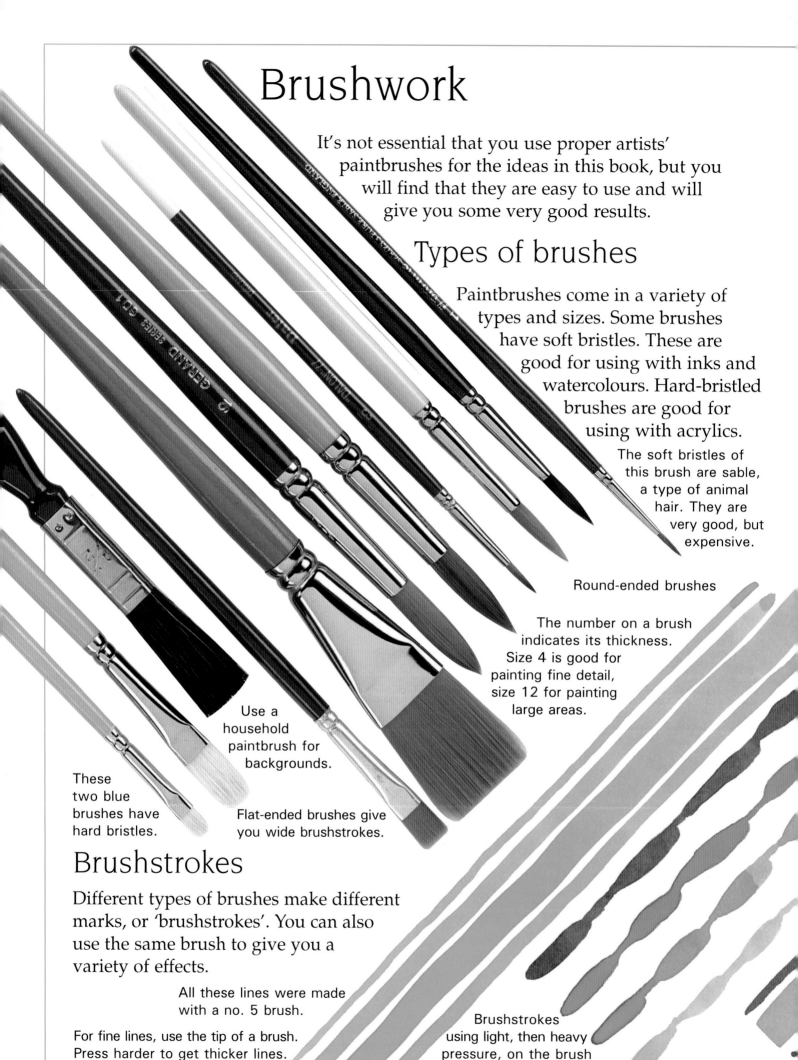

Brushwork

It's not essential that you use proper artists' paintbrushes for the ideas in this book, but you will find that they are easy to use and will give you some very good results.

Types of brushes

Paintbrushes come in a variety of types and sizes. Some brushes have soft bristles. These are good for using with inks and watercolours. Hard-bristled brushes are good for using with acrylics.

The soft bristles of this brush are sable, a type of animal hair. They are very good, but expensive.

Round-ended brushes

The number on a brush indicates its thickness. Size 4 is good for painting fine detail, size 12 for painting large areas.

Use a household paintbrush for backgrounds.

These two blue brushes have hard bristles.

Flat-ended brushes give you wide brushstrokes.

Brushstrokes

Different types of brushes make different marks, or 'brushstrokes'. You can also use the same brush to give you a variety of effects.

All these lines were made with a no. 5 brush.

For fine lines, use the tip of a brush. Press harder to get thicker lines.

Brushstrokes using light, then heavy pressure, on the brush

Looking after brushes

Don't leave brushes standing in water. This will damage the bristles.

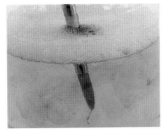

Wash brushes in warm, soapy water. Hot water loosens the bristles.

Re-shape the bristles with your fingers before they dry.

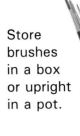

Store brushes in a box or upright in a pot.

Store brushes in a safe place where the bristles won't get damaged.

Build up patterns with different combinations of brushstrokes.

Lay the bristles flat on the paper, to make marks like these.

This chequerboard pattern was made with the tip of a flat-ended brush.

Use the tip of a fine, round brush to make small marks.

Dip pen

Chinese lettering brush

Feathers

Other 'brushes'

There are lots of other things, apart from artists' brushes which you can use to paint with. Experiment with some of the things shown here.

Piece of sponge

Cotton buds

Mixing colours

You only need a few colours of paint to be able to mix a wide range of other colours. If you are going to buy some paints, here is a suggestion of the basic colours to get.

Vermilion red - good for mixing with yellow to make orange, or with blue, to make brown

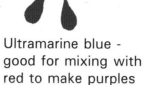

Ultramarine blue - good for mixing with red to make purples

Lemon yellow - good for mixing with blue to make greens

Yellow ochre - good for mixing with red to make earthy colours such as brown and terracotta

Prussian or cobalt blue - good for mixing with yellow to make greens

Crimson red - good for mixing with blue to make purples

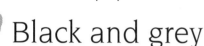

Burnt umber - mix it with blue, to get black.

White - mix it with colours to make pastel shades.

Black and grey

These paints have been darkened with black.

This blue/brown mix has been added to crimson.

You don't need black to make grey, either.

If you mix black with a colour to make it darker, the paint can look very dull. Use other colours instead to darken colours.

Instead of using black, mix ultramarine and burnt umber together. Mix in this blackish colour to darken paints.

To mix a light grey, mix blue, with white, then add a tiny amount of yellow and vermilion.

Mixing colours for skies

Blue and white

Vermilion and lemon yellow

A little orange added.

A little white added.

More blue added.

Lots more blue, red and yellow added.

Add more white.

1. Mix white and cobalt blue on your palette. Clean your brush. Mix a little vermilion and lemon yellow to make orange.

2. Add a tiny amount of the orange to the blue you have mixed. See what colour it makes. Then, try adding a little white.

3. Add different colours to the paint. Some of the colours would be good for a bright sunny sky, others for stormy skies.

Mixing skin colours

Brush the paint next to the square.

Match the colours as closely as you can.

1. Find pictures of faces in magazines. Cut a square from each one. Glue them onto paper.

2. Mix some red paint with white, then a little yellow and blue, until you've got a good match.

3. Cut out half a face from a magazine and glue it onto paper. Paint the other half, matching the colours.

Mixing greens

You may have noticed that there is no green paint in the list of recommended colours. You don't need to buy it because you can easily use other colours to mix different greens.

1. Mix together a little lemon yellow and cobalt blue to make a brightish green colour.

2. Then, add different amounts of red. See how many different greens you can make.

Acrylic paints

Acrylic paints are very bright and easy to mix. They can be used in a variety of ways to get different effects.

Using acrylics

Squeeze small blobs of acrylic paint onto an old plate or palette. Mix them with water, or use them straight from the tube. Wash your brushes well, because the paint is waterproof when it dries.

You can use the paint as it is, without mixing it with water.

Or, you can add water to the paint to make it thinner and more transparent.

Different effects

Using paint straight from the tube, try short brushstrokes with a flat-ended brush.

Paint a patch of colour in thick paint, then scratch into it with a piece of cardboard.

Cut notches in a piece of cardboard. Scrape it across the paint to make lines.

Use the pointed end of a paintbrush to scratch swirls into thick paint.

For a criss-cross effect, press the edge of a piece of thick cardboard into the paint.

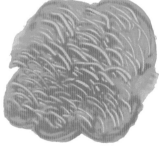

To get a textured pattern, scratch into thick paint with the prongs of a plastic fork.

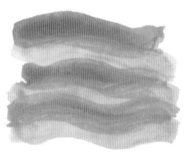

Mix paint with a little water to make it watery. Do wavy lines in different colours.

Paint lines with watery paint. Let them dry. Add shapes with thick paint on top.

This picture was created using papers decorated with patterns made in thick paint, using the techniques shown on the opposite page. Shapes were cut, then glued together to make a collage.

Thick and thin paint

THICK PAPER, SUCH AS CARTRIDGE PAPER

You can get different effects by using acrylic paint straight from a bottle or tube, or by thinning it with water. Acrylics also have an adhesive quality, so thin paper, such as tissue paper, sticks to it when the paint dries.

The background of the picture below was painted with thin paint, then patterns were added with thick paint.

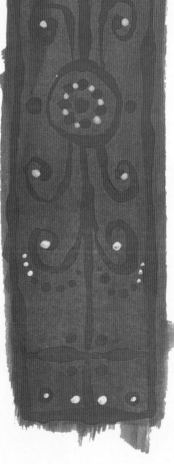

For a tartan pattern, the green and white stripes were painted with thin paint. The purple ones were thick paint.

The squares above were outlined with thin paint. Details were added with thick paint.

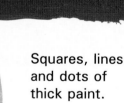

Squares, lines and dots of thick paint.

The purple flower on the right is tissue paper. Thick white paint was added on top.

The strawberry was cut from tissue paper. Thin white paint was painted on top.

Tissue prints

Red or orange tissue work best.

1. Mix some thin paint and brush it onto some paper in an even wash.

2. Cut a shape from tissue paper. Press it on the wet paint.

3. Leave the shape for a minute or so, then peel off the tissue paper.

The stripes and spots below were all painted with thick paint.

The top and bottom hearts were printed.

The flower and leaf on the left are tissue paper with thick paint on top.

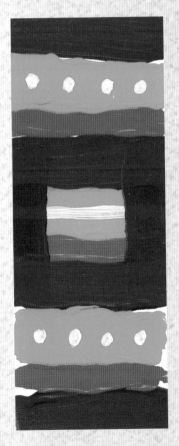 

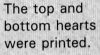

The details on the dog and the fish were added with a felt-tip, once the paint had dried.

A tissue paper heart with thick paint on top.

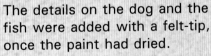

Patterns and dots

LARGE PIECE OF CARTRIDGE PAPER

Mix the paints in a plastic container.

1. Mix red and yellow acrylic paints to make orange, then add blue to make rust.

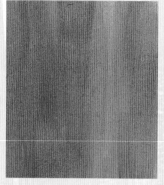

2. Paint a large piece of paper all over with the rust paint. Use a thick paintbrush.

3. When the rust paint has dried, paint a large black snake curling around the paper.

4. Use yellow ochre to paint a circle in the middle of the snake. Let it dry.

5. Cut a piece of sponge cloth for the bottom of three more pots. Dampen the cloth slightly.

6. Spread the sponge cloths with some black, ochre and white paint.

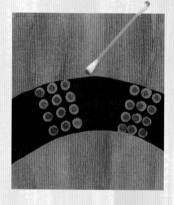

7. Press a cotton bud onto the ochre sponge. Print lines of dots on the snake.

8. Use another cotton bud to fill in between the lines with rows of rust dots.

9. Add white dots around the outline of the snake. Space the dots evenly.

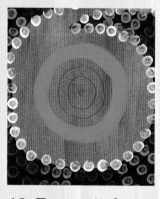

10. Draw circles inside the ochre one. Use these as guides to print white dots.

11. Print black and white flowers around the ochre circle. Fill in with ochre dots.

12. Print white and ochre flowers around the snake. Fill the background with black dots.

14

Glue pictures

A PIECE OF CARDBOARD

This idea uses PVA glue for drawing, which leaves a raised line when it dries. The raised lines are then covered with gold acrylic paint and black shoe polish is rubbed in to get an 'antique' look.

You will need a bottle of PVA glue which has a nozzle top.

Test it on newspaper.

1. If the glue is new, snip a little piece off the nozzle. Test it to see the thickness of the line it makes.

2. If the line you have drawn is very thin, snip a little bit more off the end of the nozzle.

3. Draw a simple picture on the cardboard. Place the nozzle of the glue where you want to start.

4. Then, draw around your picture, squeezing the glue out gently as you draw.

5. When you get to the end of a line, lift the glue up quickly, so that it doesn't drip.

6. Add some wavy lines, swirls and dots on the cardboard, around your drawing.

7. Leave it to dry overnight. Then, paint all over with gold acrylic paint. Let the paint dry.

8. To get the antique look, put some black shoe polish on a soft cloth, then rub it all over.

Cut the cardboard into different shapes, before decorating it.

Make a frame for a picture or photo.

Printing patterns

ANY PAPER

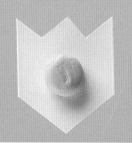

Spread the paint with the back of a spoon.

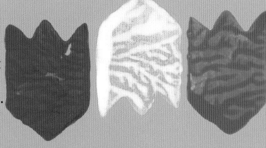

Press firmly.

1. Draw a simple shape on a piece of cardboard. Cut it out.

2. Press a lump of poster putty onto the back, to make a handle.

3. Squeeze paint onto newspaper. Spread the paint with a spoon.

4. Press the shape into the paint, then print it on some paper.

Printing patterns

Experiment with making different patterns. Try printing rows or joining up the prints.

Press the cardboard into the paint before you do each print.

Two-tone prints

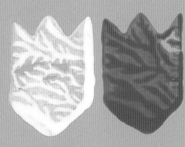

Cut different shapes and print them as part of your pattern.

For a two-tone print, spread two colours of paint on the newspaper.

Press the shape into the paint where the two colours meet.

Straight lines

The effect you get depends on the thickness of the cardboard.

Thin cardboard

Thick cardboard

Corrugated cardboard

1. Cut different thicknesses of cardboard into thin strips.

2. Dip the edge of the cardboard into the paint, then print a line.

Cut out and print a fish shape. Add details with the edge of small strips of cardboard.

Curved shapes

Dip the edge of a piece of cardboard into paint. Bend it as you print.

For a spiral, print curved shapes, joining them in the middle.

For a looped pattern, bend some thin cardboard and secure it with tape.

More printed patterns

Twist this end.

1. To make a fan shape, dip the edge of a piece of cardboard into some paint.

2. Twist the top of the cardboard as you print, keeping the bottom corner in one place.

Do several fan shapes to make a flower.

Experiment with lots of different patterns and shapes.

Use the edge of cardboard for a stem. Print a small triangle for petals.

For a flower
like the one
above, overlap
three prints.

Dip a loop of cardboard
in two colours of paint
(see pages 18 and 19)
for a flower like this.

Ready-mix and poster paints

Ready-mix paints and poster paints are good for simple, bold pictures, although poster paints tend to give much brighter results than ready-mix paints. Both types of paint can be thinned with water.

Squeeze ready-mix onto a palette before you use it. Be careful if you mix these paints, as the colours can look dull when they dry. Poster paints can be used straight from the pot, or mix them with each other on a palette. The picture on the opposite page includes some colours which were mixed.

It's best to use thick cartridge paper with these paints. Thinner paper will go crinkly.

Poster paints are sold in little pots and are more expensive than ready-mix paints.

The picture below had outlines added with a felt-tip pen, once the paint was dry.

Elastic band prints

THICK CARDBOARD

1. Use a ballpoint pen to draw a simple design on a piece of thick cardboard.

2. Paint over the cardboard with a thick layer of PVA glue. Wash your brush.

3. Cut pieces of a thick elastic band to fit the main shapes. Press them on firmly.

4. Cut pieces of a narrower elastic band for the details. Press them onto the glue.

  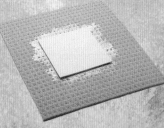 

5. Cut squares from a thick elastic band. Press them onto the background.

6. When the glue has dried, paint some ready-mix paint onto a sponge cloth.

7. Put the cardboard, picture-side down, into the paint. Press on the back firmly.

8. Lay the painted cardboard on a pad of newspaper. Press all over the back, then lift it off.

9. Do several practice prints like this before doing a 'proper' print on paper.

Experiment by printing on different colours of paper.

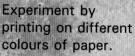   

Prints on tissue paper

These prints work particularly well on bright tissue paper. Follow the steps below.

1. If you want to print on tissue paper, press the cardboard in some paint.

2. Carefully lay the painted cardboard, face-up, on a pile of newspaper.

Different colours printed on tissue paper

3. Lay a double layer of tissue paper on top and press gently. Peel it off carefully.

Use thick and thin elastic bands for a flower, like this.

For a multi-coloured print, paint the elastic bands with different colours.

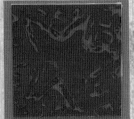

Gold acrylic paint on dark purple paper

Hand and cardboard prints

ANY LIGHT-COLOURED PAPER

Turn over to page 28 to see a full-size version of the prints shown on these two pages.

You'll need to be near a sink and have lots of paper towels to wipe your hands.

1. For the background, brush some plastic foodwrap with blue paint.

2. Lay some paper on top of it and press lightly. Lift off the paper and leave it to dry.

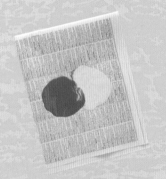

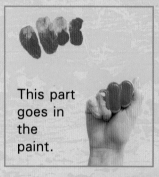

This part goes in the paint.

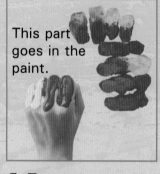

This part goes in the paint.

3. For a seahorse, pour two shades of ready-mix or poster paint onto a pad of newspapers.

4. For the head, press the top of your fingers into the paint. Print them on the paper.

5. Press your knuckles into the paint. Turn your hand sideways and print a body.

6. Put paint on your little finger as far as your knuckle. Print a long snout with it.

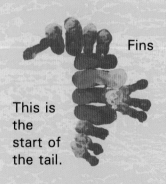

This is the start of the tail.

Fins

Do smaller and smaller prints.

7. Use the same finger to print three fins and three more prints below the body.

8. Use a fingertip to add two prints at the end of the snout. Print some along the head.

9. Finish the tail by doing several prints with a fingertip. Curve them around.

10. Dip a fingertip in a bright colour and print an eye. Add the middle when it's dry.

Crabs

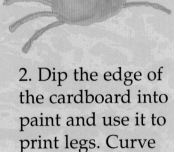
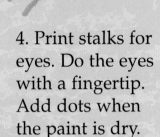

1. Print the crab's body with your thumb. Cut a piece of thin cardboard, about 3cm long.

2. Dip the edge of the cardboard into paint and use it to print legs. Curve it as you print.

3. Use a small piece of cardboard to print V-shaped pincers on the front legs.

4. Print stalks for eyes. Do the eyes with a fingertip. Add dots when the paint is dry.

Fan fish

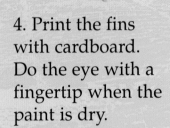

1. Dip the edge of a piece of thin cardboard into two or three colours of paint.

2. Press it onto your paper, then twist one end to make a fan shape. Turn the paper.

3. Print another fan to finish the body. Then print a narrower one for the tail.

4. Print the fins with cardboard. Do the eye with a fingertip when the paint is dry.

Little rainbow fish

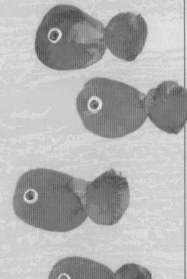
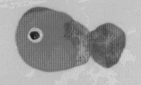
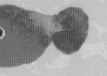

1. Press the fat part of your thumb into several colours of paint. Print it.

2. Add a tail with a fingertip. For the eye, dip the end of an old pencil in paint, then print it.

The instructions for these prints are on pages 26-27.

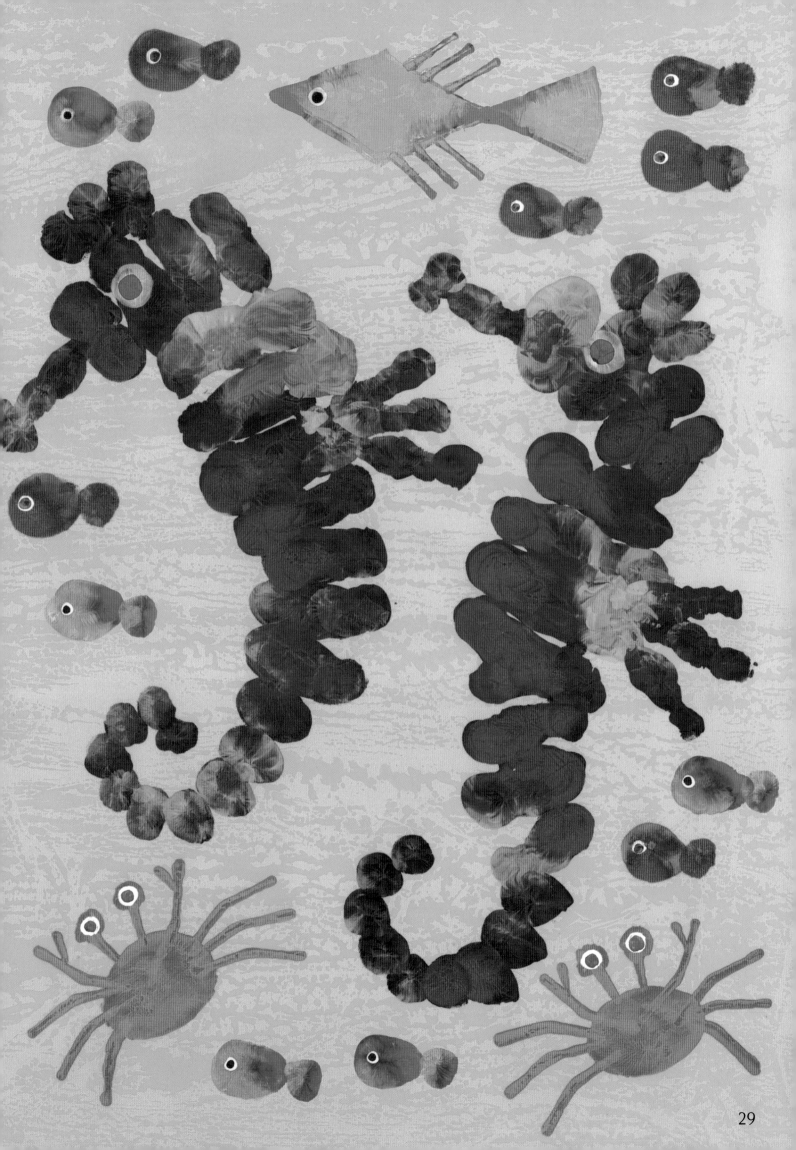

Masking out and spattering

A COLOURED PIECE OF PAPER AND ANOTHER PIECE THE SAME SIZE.

  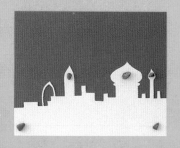 

1. Put the coloured paper to one side. Draw an outline on the other piece. Cut it out.

2. Lay newspapers outside. Put small stones around the edge to weight them down.

3. Put the coloured paper on the newspapers, with the cut-out on top. Weight it down.

4. Pour some ready-mix paint into a yogurt pot. Add water to make it runny.

 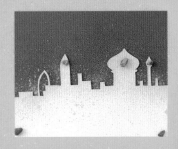  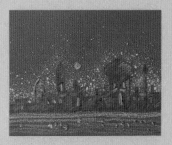

5. Dip a toothbrush into the paint. Pull a ruler along the bristles <u>towards</u> you to splatter the paint.

6. Carry on spattering paint around the cut-out until the speckles are quite dense.

7. Lift the paper cut-out to leave the area you masked out. Leave it to dry.

8. Add details and shading such as windows and a watery reflection, with pastels.

Pulled cardboard prints

USE THICK CARDBOARD

 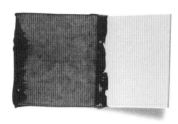  

1. Put some paint on a plate. Dip the edge of a piece of cardboard into it.

2. Put the painted edge onto your paper and pull it evenly to the side.

3. Dip the edge in the paint again then, pull it towards you.

4. For a diamond shape, pull the card diagonally out to one side.

Use a different piece of cardboard for each colour you use.

 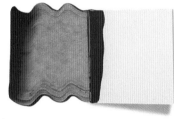

Keep the edge vertical.

5. For a zigzag effect pull the edge diagonally down then up.

6. For a wiggly line, pull the edge to one side in a wavy motion.

Print a tree with several overlapping curves.

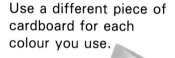

Zigzag roofs

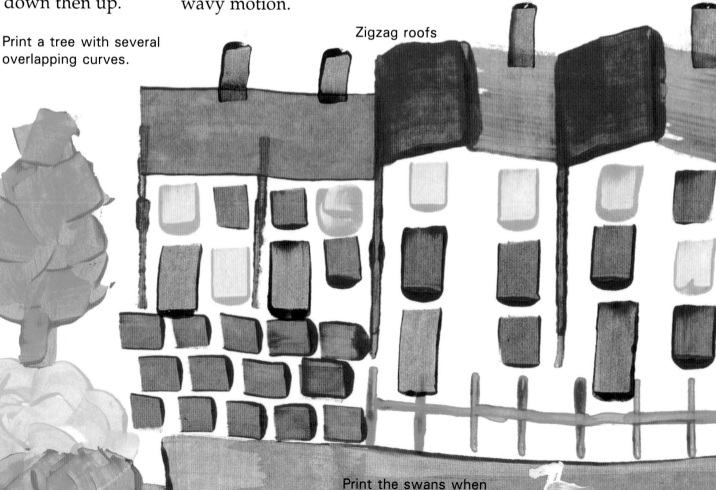

Print the swans when the water is dry.

Swans and ducks

Bricks

Start here.

1. Dip the edge of a piece of cardboard in paint and print a line.

2. Move the edge below the line and pull the edge in a wavy line.

3. Use the edge of a piece of cardboard for the head and beak.

Print in rows with narrow cardboard in a darker shade of paint.

For hills, do long wavy prints with a wide piece of cardboard. Make them overlap.

Paint and tissue paper

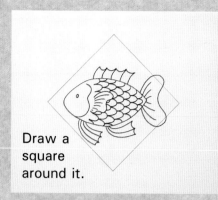

Draw a square around it.

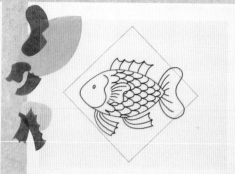

1. Use a thick black felt-tip pen to draw a bold drawing of a fish. Do it on white paper.

2. Trace the main shapes of your fish onto different colours of tissue paper, then cut them out.

Use your picture as a guide.

3. Cut a piece of polythene from a clear plastic bag. Make sure it is bigger than your drawing.

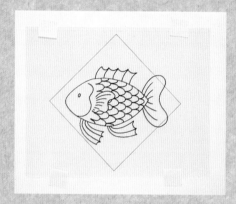

4. Lay the polythene over your drawing. Put pieces of tape along the edges to secure it.

5. Brush the tissue paper shapes with PVA glue. Press each one in place onto the polythene.

6. Cut or tear strips of tissue paper for the background. Glue them on around the fish.

7. Glue a piece of pale blue tissue paper over the whole picture, then leave it to dry.

8. When the glue is completely dry, carefully peel the tissue paper off the polythene.

9. Place the tissue paper over your drawing. Go over your outlines using black paint.

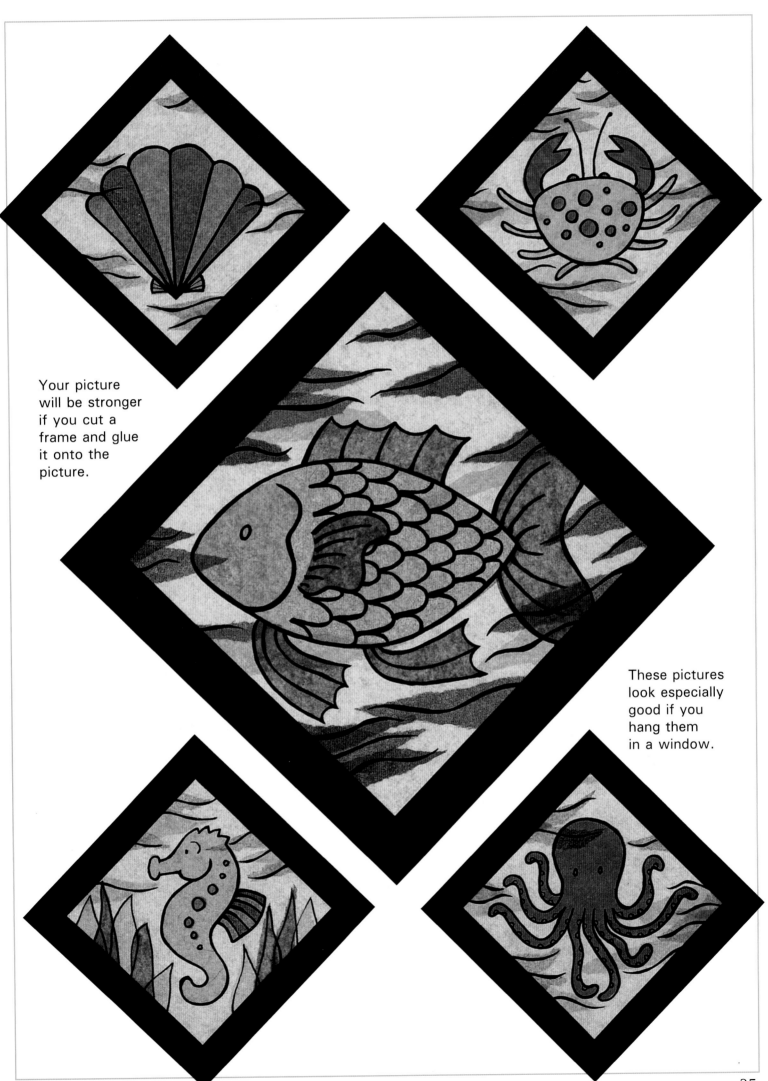

Your picture will be stronger if you cut a frame and glue it onto the picture.

These pictures look especially good if you hang them in a window.

35

About colours

Which colours go well together? Why do some colours appear to jump out of a painting and some seem to blend in with the colours around them. These pages show how different combinations of colours alter the way a painting looks.

Primary colours

There are three colours which cannot be made by mixing other colours. These are red, yellow and blue, and they are known as primary colours.

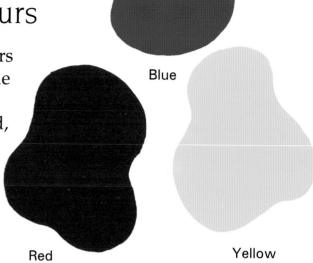

Blue

Red

Yellow

Secondary colours

If you mix each of the primary colours with another one, you get orange, green and purple. These are known as secondary colours.

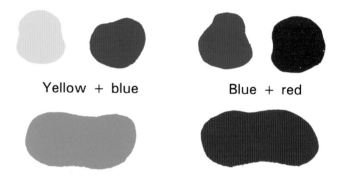

Red + yellow

Yellow + blue

Blue + red

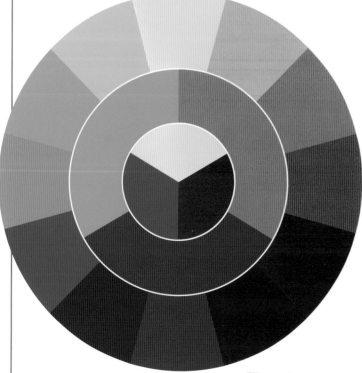

The secondary colours are in the middle ring of the colour circle.

The primary colours are in the centre of the colour circle.

More colours

You can get more colours by mixing a primary with a secondary colour. These mixes are shown on the outside ring of the colour circle.

If you mix yellow with orange you get a colour between the two.

Blue mixed with green makes a bluey-green.

Red and orange make an orangey-red.

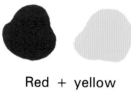
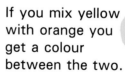

Harmonic colours

Harmonic colours are those which lie near each other on the outside ring of the colour circle, such as blue, light blue, green and light green.

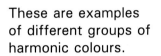

These are examples of different groups of harmonic colours.

Complementary colours

The colours which lie diagonally opposite each other in the colour circle are called complementary colours. They have most contrast when they are painted next to each other.

When you paint complementary colours next to each other they 'buzz' and make your eyes bounce.

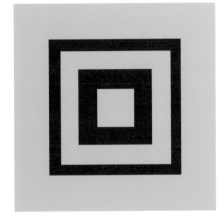

Warm and cool colours

Some colours give the feeling of warmth or coldness and are actually known as warm or cool colours. Warm colours look brighter and stand out more in a picture than cool colours.

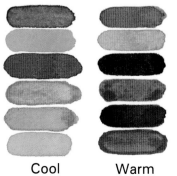

Cool colours   Warm colours

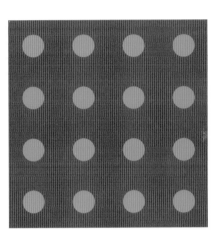

The cool colours used in this picture give it a cold, icy feeling.

Colour and tone

The tone of a colour is how light or dark it is. You can create unusual pictures by painting in tones of one colour or by changing the tones in a picture.

This circle shows the tones of different colours.

Yellow is the lightest tone.

Green is a middle tone.

Blue is a dark tone.

Orange is a light tone too.

Red is a middle tone.

Purple is a dark tone.

Experimenting with tones

Experiment with making as many different tones of one colour as you can. Always start with the lightest tone and get gradually darker. This is easiest to do with acrylic, poster or ready-mix paints.

All these tones were made by adding a colour to white.

Start with white. Add a tiny amount of a colour.

Add more and more of the colour until you get a dark tone.

Light and dark tones

The tones in a picture can change the feeling or mood of it. Light tones give a soft, pastel effect, whereas dark tones make a picture look stronger.

Compare the picture at the top, which is painted using light tones only, with the one at the bottom, which is painted in darker tones.

Similar tones

Although colours look very different they can have the same tones. It's easiest to see the similarities between colours in a black and white picture.

Compare the tones in the colour and the black and white photographs. For instance, the red paper and blue squares have a similar tone.

The flowers have the lightest tone. The purple squares on the paper have the darkest tone.

In this black and white photograph it's easier to see which colours have a similar tone.

Reversing tones

You can get some surprising effects if you reverse the order of tones, so that yellow becomes the darkest tone and blue becomes the lightest one.

The tones in the second picture below have been reversed. Any part of the picture which was a dark colour has become lighter.

Light blue has become dark blue.

Inks

Inks are ideal for painting or drawing bright, vibrant pictures. Use them with a brush, a dip pen or draw with a cartridge pen. They are also ideal for resist techniques with wax crayons (see page 76) or oil pastels.

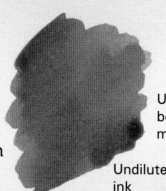

Use straight from a bottle or cartridge pen or mix them with water.

Undiluted ink

Watered-down ink.

Paint ink over oil pastels or wax crayons for a resist effect.

Ink blobs

Wet a piece of watercolour paper then drop spots of inks on it. When the paper is dry, draw on top with a felt-tip or dip pen.

Try doing blobs close together. Let the colours bleed into each other.

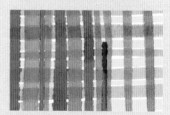

Stripes

The colours change where they overlap.

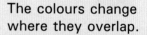

1. On dry paper, paint stripes of different colours. Vary the thickness.

2. When the ink is dry, brush stripes across the other stripes.

Spooky trees

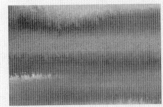

1. Paint a wash with watercolour paints (see page 48). Leave it to dry.

2. Paint a line of black ink. Use a straw to blow the ink into shapes.

Scratched resist

1. Use a pencil to draw a random pattern all over a piece of paper.

2. Draw a line next to the ones already drawn to make double lines.

3. Fill in the shapes using oil pastels. Try not to go over the lines.

4. Brush black drawing ink all over the paper. Leave it to dry.

Use the corner of a screwdriver to scrape the patterns.

5. Scrape a pattern through the ink to reveal the colour underneath.

6. Carry on scraping different patterns into all the shapes.

Warning!

Inks will stain your clothes, so always wear something to protect you when you use them. Don't forget to rinse your brush or dip pen, too.

Brush and ink paintings

ANY THICK WHITE PAPER

The best kind of brush to use for pictures like these, are soft-haired brushes which have a pointed tip. Chinese or Japanese lettering brushes are ideal for these techniques.

Use a soft brush with a pointed tip.

Mixing the inks

To do the paintings on these pages, you need to use three shades of one colour of ink. Use ink from a bottle or snip the end off an ink cartridge.

Add a few drops of ink to water in a small container to make a watery ink.

Mix a medium shade, by adding more drops of ink to water in another container.

Undiluted ink. Use straight from a bottle or squeeze the ink from a cartridge into a container.

Bamboo

Practise on scrap paper before doing a large picture.

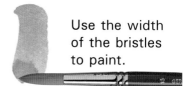

Use the width of the bristles to paint.

Don't put more ink on your brush.

Use the tip of the brush to begin with, then increase the pressure.

1. Dip your brush in the watery ink, then dab the bristles on a paper towel. Paint a section of a stem.

2. Paint another two sections above the first one. Leave a small space between each section.

3. Using the medium ink and the tip of your brush, add branches coming out from the stem.

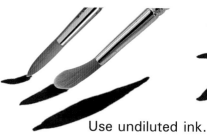

Use undiluted ink.

Press lightly.

4. Add twigs onto the branches. Leave a small space between one twig and the next one.

5. For a leaf, press lightly on the tip of the brush, then press a little harder then press lightly again.

6. Use the tip of the brush and undiluted ink to paint grass and lines at the joints on the stem.

Bird

For each line, start with the tip, then press harder, then lighter again.

1. Using undiluted ink, paint the beak with the tip of your brush. Add the neck and body.

2. Paint the head, an eye and a line for the bird's back. Add a branch at the bottom of the body.

Make the lines different lengths.

3. For a tail, paint several lines joining on to the body.

Brush paintings

WATERCOLOUR OR CARTRIDGE PAPER

All the pictures on these pages were painted using three shades of ink. You paint the main shapes, then details are added with a very fine brush or dip pen. Before you begin, follow the steps on page 42 for mixing the ink.

Bugs

1. Use the medium ink to paint a body. Add wings with the watery ink.

2. Add a head, eyes, antennae and legs with undiluted ink.

Fish

1. Use the very watery ink to paint a simple shape of a fish.

2. Add the head, gills and underside of the fish with the medium ink.

3. Use a pen or fine brush and undiluted ink to add an outline.

4. Add an eye, mouth, fins and a tail with the undiluted ink.

Paint a lily pad with different shades of ink.

For a background like this, paint a watercolour wash (see page 48). Let it dry before adding the creatures.

Use the tip of a thin brush to paint reeds.

Frog

1. Use the very watery ink to paint a shape for the body.

2. Use the tip of the brush to add a darker stripe along the shape with the medium ink.

3. Before the body has dried, add some spots of the medium ink to it.

4. Use undiluted ink to draw an eye. Outline the body and add a leg.

Watercolour paints

Watercolour paints can give you bright, vibrant colours, but they are also particularly good for painting skies and water.

Paints

Most watercolour paints are sold in tubes or as small, solid blocks, called pans. The pans are easy to use and are more economical.

The paint in tubes is quite thick. Mix it with water on a palette.

Boxes of watercolours are filled with pans or half-pans. You can buy each colour separately.

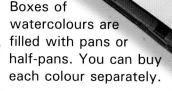

Half-pans of watercolour paints

Watercolour paper

Watercolour paper comes in different thicknesses and with different textures. You can buy it from art shops in blocks, spiral-bound pads and as individual sheets.

The thickness of the paper is shown by its weight. Look for paper which is 190gsm (90lb) or above. It won't wrinkle too much when you paint on it.

The paper in watercolour blocks is glued around the edges. Slip a blunt knife into the gap. Gently cut the piece of paper away from the block.

Rough watercolour paper has most texture.

Hot-pressed or Smooth paper has the smoothest surface.

'Not' or cold-pressed paper has a semi-rough texture.

A block of watercolour paper

Most of the watercolour projects in this book were done on 'not' paper.

Mixing watercolours

If you have tubes of watercolour paints, mix them in the same ways as you would mix acrylics. Find out how to do this on page 10. These steps show you how to mix paint from pans.

1. Dip your brush in water, then blot it on a paper towel to get rid of some of the water.

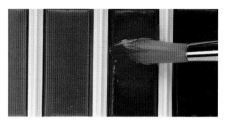

2. Move the brush around and around in one colour until the bristles are covered in paint.

3. Dab the paint onto a palette, then repeat the steps to make a larger patch of colour.

4. Rinse and blot your brush on a paper towel, then dip it into the colour you want to mix in.

5. Mix this paint with the first colour on the palette. Repeat until you get the colour you want.

Watercolour paints look darker when they are wet. They become lighter once they are dry.

Prussian blue

All these colours were made by mixing Prussian blue and carmine.

If you want to mix alot of one colour, put a little water into a container and mix the paint into it.

Carmine

Experimenting with watercolours

WATERCOLOUR PAPER

Watercolours can be used in lots of different ways. Experiment with these techniques on pieces of scrap watercolour paper.

Painting a wash

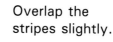

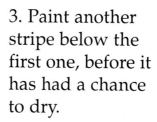

Overlap the stripes slightly.

1. Mix up plenty of paint in a container. You need enough to cover your paper.

2. Use a thick brush to paint a broad stripe across the top of the paper.

3. Paint another stripe below the first one, before it has had a chance to dry.

4. Carry on adding more stripes down the paper until it is covered.

Lifting off paint

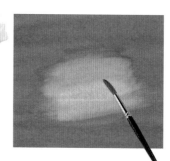

Before the paint dries in your wash, use a cotton bud to lift off some paint.

Lift off some of the paint with a scrunched up tissue. This gives a different effect.

You can also lift off paint with a clean brush. Dry it on a paper towel first.

Try using a clean sponge too. If you dab it on the paint, you get a textured effect.

Wet paper effects

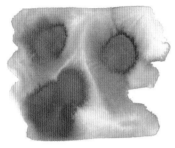

Wet a piece of paper with a sponge or thick brush. Paint small blobs on it.

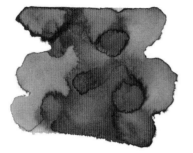

Try the same thing but use two colours. The colours will bleed into each other.

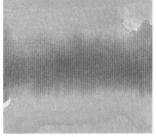

Paint a wash in one colour. Before it dries, paint a stripe in a different colour.

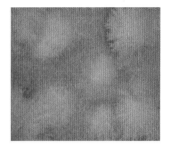

Paint a wash. Drop blobs of clean water onto the paint and let it spread.

Colour blends

1. Wipe a clean, wet sponge across your paper to make it wet.

2. Mix two different colours of watercolours on a palette.

3. Cover about a third of the paper with a wash in one colour.

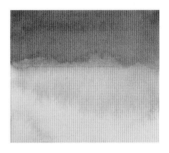

4. Turn the paper upside down and paint on a second wash of colour.

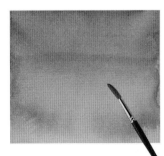

5. Brush across the paper to blend the colours where they meet.

Try blending three colours together.

This picture has a colour-blended sky. The trees were painted on wet paper.

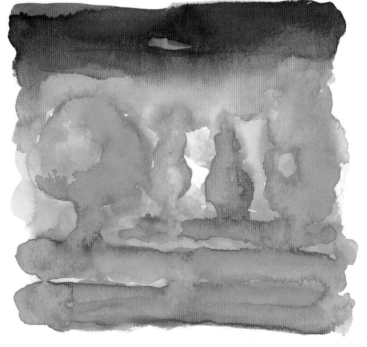

Painting on wet paper

WATERCOLOUR PAPER

Before you do the project on these pages, try out this technique on some spare scrap paper.

1. Put three colours of watercolour paint on a palette.

2. Use a sponge or a big clean brush to paint water all over the paper.

The paint will spread.

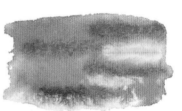

3. Brush short, light strokes of colour onto the wet paper.

Experiment with different combinations of colours.

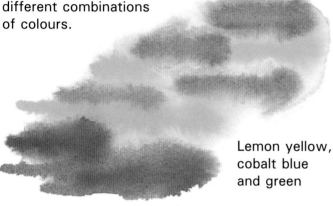

Lemon yellow, cobalt blue and green

Let the second colour run into the first one.

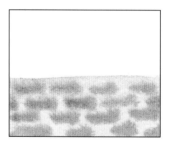

4. Wet another piece of paper. Use two different colours of paint.

5. Try another sample with three colours of paint. Let the colours run.

Windmills and a canal

1. Mix patches of two different blues and green watercolour paint.

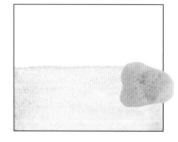

2. Use a sponge or a clean brush to wet the bottom half of the paper.

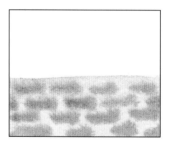

3. Brush short, strokes of one of the blues, all over the wet area.

4. Add strokes of the other blue and green. Let them run into each other.

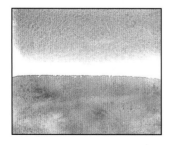

5. Wet the paper at the top. Paint a pale blue wash for the sky.

6. When the paint has dried, paint a green stripe and windmill shapes.

7. Use the tip of a thin brush to add lines for the windmills' sails.

8. Use green to paint the leaves in the foreground. Add red tulips.

The sea in these pictures was painted first, then the sky was added. Details were added with watercolours once the background had dried.

Water painting
WATERCOLOUR OR THICK CARTRIDGE PAPER

This is another idea which shows how watercolour paints spread on wet paper.

Before you start, mix a tiny amount of blue paint with a little water to make a very watery paint.

The paint spreads up to the outline.

1. Paint the outline of a simple shape with the watery paint. Fill in the shape with water.

2. Mix some other colours. While the shape is still wet, paint a blob of colour inside it.

3. Add other blobs of colour so that they run together. Leave it flat to dry.

Paint the trunk of the tree first, then the leaves.

Paint the butterfly's feelers with a thin brush.

Use greens and
blues for the lower
leaves. Paint red,
yellow and orange
leaves near the top.

Blow paintings

ANY KIND OF THICK PAPER

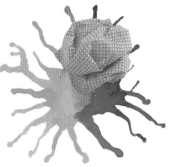

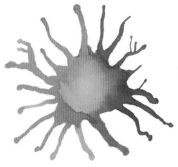

The colours will mix.

1. Mix two colours of paint with water. Make them runny.

2. Pour some of each colour onto paper, close together.

3. Place a straw above the middle of the paint and blow very hard.

4. As you blow, 'chase' the paint outwards to make spiky shapes.

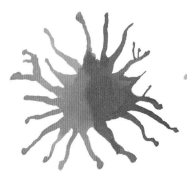

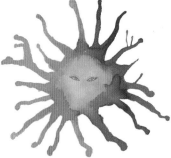

5. Keep on blowing the paint out in different directions.

6. Gently blot the middle of the paint with the corner of a damp rag.

7. Then, go around and around wiping the paint into the shape of a face.

8. Leave to dry. Then, paint eyes on the face with a fine brush.

9. Paint eyebrows and a nose. Add thin lips and spiky ears.

Use contrasting colours, such as blue and green, red and orange or red and purple.

54

Painting skies

WATERCOLOUR PAPER

Watercolours are very good for painting skies and clouds. Before painting a picture experiment with some of the ideas shown here. Use different shades of blue to suggest different types of skies.

Cloudy sky

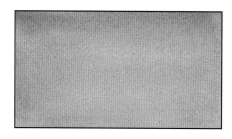

1. Wet the paper with a sponge or brush. Paint a wash of cobalt blue.

2. For fluffy clouds, use the corner of a tissue to dab off patches of paint.

Different types of sky

Paint a wash with two shades of blue for a 'heavy' sky.

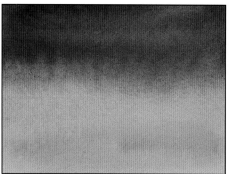

Paint a yellow and orange wash.

Add the trees when the wash has dried.

For rain clouds, dab off paint, then add a darker line along the bottom of each cloud.

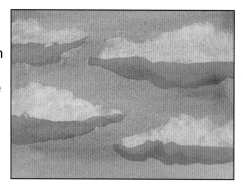

Paint a purple wash, then dab off colour with a tissue and a brush.

A stormy sky

These steps show you how to paint a dark, stormy sky.

You will need Prussian blue, burnt umber and yellow ochre watercolours for this picture.

1. Use a thick brush or clean sponge to wet the paper all over.

2. Mix Prussian blue with burnt umber to make dark grey.

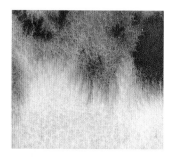

3. Blob the grey paint in patches onto the top part of the paper.

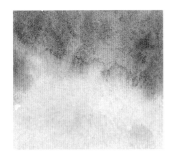

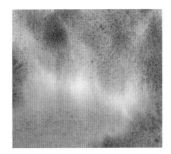

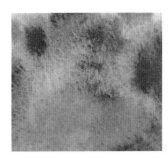

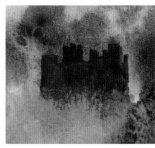

4. Add some patches of yellow ochre with the tip of your brush.

5. Mix different shades of green (see page 9). Add them at the bottom.

6. Carry on adding more greens. Let them bleed into the grey sky.

7. Let the sky dry a little, then paint a castle, using the grey from step 2.

Salt paintings

WATERCOLOUR PAPER

If you sprinkle salt onto watercolour paint, the salt soaks up the colour, and leaves a grainy effect when it dries.

Paint quickly, as the paint has to be wet when you sprinkle on the salt.

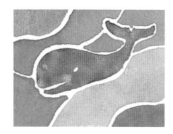

1. Paint a whale, then paint stripes for the sea, leaving a space between the stripes.

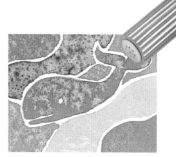

2. Before the paint has dried, sprinkle lots of salt all over the piece of paper.

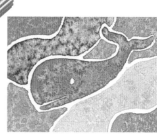

3. As the paint dries, it soaks up the salt. Leave the paint and salt to dry.

4. Shake off any excess salt, then either rub off all the salt or leave some of it on.

The salt has been left on this painting, giving the background a sandy, textured effect.

Paint things around the whale. Keep their shapes simple.

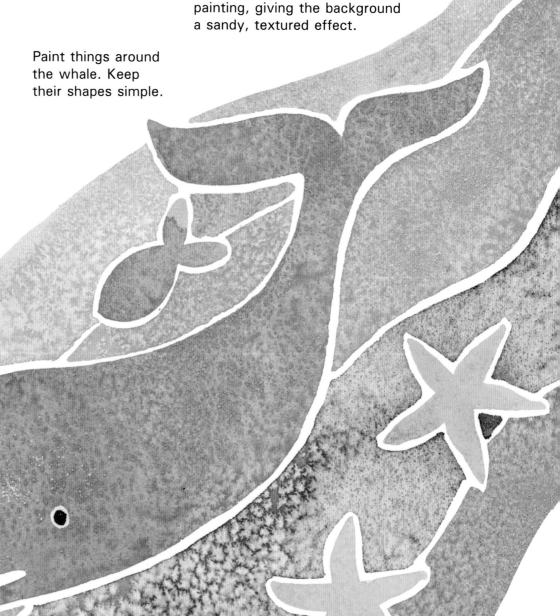

Adding highlights

Highlights make pictures come to life. They can also make things look shiny, as if they are made of glass or metal. Here are two ways of adding highlights. If you are painting with watercolours, always do the highlights by leaving a space.

Adding highlights make things such as this bird's eye, look shiny.

Paper highlights

1. Draw two circles. Fill in the inner one, leaving a small diamond-shaped space. Paint around the outside of the larger circle.

2. Use darker paint to outline the eye. Go over the inner circle, leaving another space beside the first one.

3. Fill the eye with orange paint. Add blueish-grey lines below the eye to give the eye socket some shape.

Adding white

1. Draw a robot's body. Paint over your drawing with black paint.

2. Add some white paint to the black. Paint lines inside all the shapes.

3. Mix in some more white paint. Fill in the parts shown here.

4. Wash your brush well, then add white lines inside each shape.

White can be added to any colour to make highlights.

This background was painted with very watery acrylic paint. The robots were added on top when the paint had dried.

Painting perspective

Painting pictures in perspective means doing them the way your eye sees them. Colours appear to fade the further away they are. Use any kind of paint and thick paper for painting the pictures on these pages.

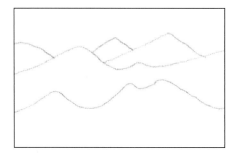

1. Draw outlines of hills in pencil. Start with the one closest to you.

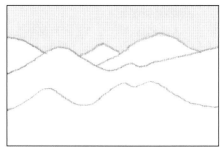

2. Mix a little blue and a spot of red with some water. Fill in the sky.

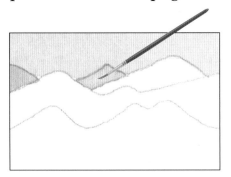

3. Add a little more blue to the paint. Fill in the furthest hills.

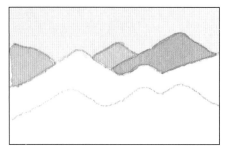

4. Add more blue and red to make the paint darker. Fill in the next hill.

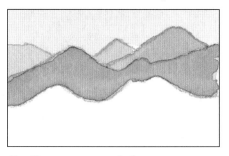

5. Carry on adding more blue and red paint until all the hills are filled in.

This picture was painted in watercolours on watercolour paper.

This picture was created by painting the houses, sea, curtain and hills first. The window frame and cat were painted once the rest were dry.

Chalk pastels

Chalk pastels, or soft pastels, are very soft and they smudge easily. This means that you can get some great effects by mixing and blending them.

Hold a pastel like a pencil and use the end to draw marks like the zigzags, above.

Lay the pastel flat on the paper.

You can also draw with the side of a pastel. Snap it in half and peel off any paper.

Mixing colours

You can mix pastels on your paper by doing strokes one on top of the other.

Experiment with the order in which you use the pastels. Do you get different colours?

Blending

1. You can also blend pastels. Draw overlapping strokes in different colours.

2. Then, smudge the colours together with a finger. This gives a soft effect.

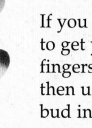

If you don't want to get your fingers messy, then use a cotton bud instead.

Graduating colours

The colours mix in the middle.

1. Starting at the top, use the side of a pastel to do strokes across your paper.

2. Do more strokes, with another pastel. Overlap some of the first colour.

Broken colours

1. Start in the middle. Draw lots of short strokes in one colour around a central point.

2. Fill in some of the spaces with other short strokes in different colours.

Dotted pictures

 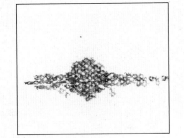  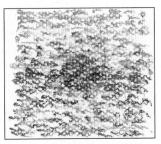

1. Use the end of orange and red pastels to draw short strokes for a sun.

2. Draw a line of light blue and dark blue strokes across the middle of the sun.

3. Draw yellow and orange strokes around the sun. Add some in the sky.

4. Use different shades of blue for the sky and the sea. Add pink strokes too.

Paper for pastels

You can get some good effects with pastels if you draw on coloured paper. For the best results, use paper which has a slightly rough or textured surface.

The paper below is called Ingres paper. Art shops and stationers sell it.

Pastels work very well on black paper.

Sugar paper is good and it's also cheap.

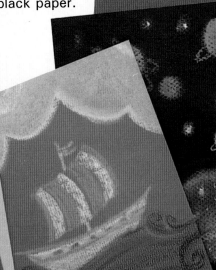

A pastel fantasy landscape

CARTRIDGE PAPER

1. Draw two curved bands, using a black chalk pastel.

2. Fill in the space between the bands with a dark blue pastel.

3. Add a band of yellow, then another band of dark blue.

4. Fill in with diagonal strokes of black and ultramarine blue.

5. Do long white strokes on top of the bands of black, to make grey.

6. Blend all the colours with your finger or a cotton bud (see page 64).

7. Wash your hands or use several cotton buds. They will get dirty.

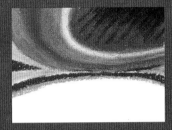

8. Draw a grey line across your paper. Add red and yellow stripes above it.

9. Draw different sizes of circles and lots of wavy lines in the foreground.

The paper protects your picture.

10. Lay a piece of scrap paper over the bottom part of your picture.

11. Draw moons and stars in the sky. Then gently blend them in.

12. Draw clouds on the horizon with grey or a mixture of black and white.

13. Use yellow to add a wavy highlight along each cloud.

14. Blend the foreground, but leave the clouds as they are.

More chalk techniques

These pages show you two more techniques for mixing colours with chalk pastels. In both techniques, you don't rub the colours to blend them; the colours mix where they overlap.

Experiment with different shapes, patterns and colours.

Remember the colour of the paper you draw on affects the colours the pastels make.

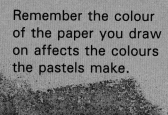

Blocking

Use the side of a chalk pastel to fill in areas of colour. This is known as blocking. Then go over the top with another colour of pastel.

Hatching

Use the end of a pastel to build up layers of short diagonal lines. Try using different combinations of colours.

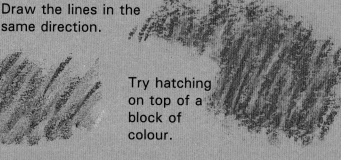

Draw the lines in the same direction.

Try hatching on top of a block of colour.

Landscape

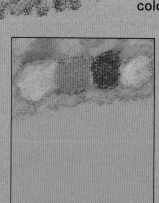

1. Use the side of a turquoise chalk pastel to block in the sky. Leave gaps for the trees.

2. Add patches of pale blue to the sky. Then, some dark blue over the top.

3. Use the side of red, yellow and orange pastels to fill in the shape of the trees.

4. Add hatching on top of each tree with different colours. Let them merge together.

5. Use the side of green, yellow and orange pastels to add stripes below the sky.

6. Add hatching on top of the stripes. Make them get longer in the foreground.

7. Use the end of a black pastel to draw a line below the trees. Add branches, too.

Oil pastels

Oil pastels give you very bright, strong colours. They don't smudge in the way chalk pastels do. This makes them easier to use. You can do lots of the same things with oil pastels that you can do with chalk pastels.

Like chalk pastels, oil pastels work well on coloured paper which has a slightly textured surface.

Try doing short strokes in the same direction in different colours.

Use them on their side to fill in areas of colour. Peel off the paper and break them in half, first.

Try doing lots of overlapping strokes in different colours.

A white oil pastel shows up well on brightly coloured paper.

You can draw on black paper with oil pastels, although the colours you get may change slightly.

Mixing colours

To mix colours, use one colour on top of another (see the tiger opposite). The colours blend together.

Oil pastels work well on cartridge paper and sugar paper.

A tiger in long grass

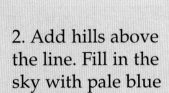
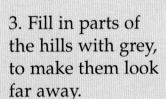
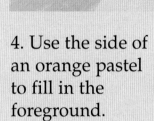

1. Draw a straight purple line about a third of the way down the paper.

2. Add hills above the line. Fill in the sky with pale blue and white.

3. Fill in parts of the hills with grey, to make them look far away.

4. Use the side of an orange pastel to fill in the foreground.

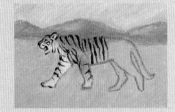

5. Draw the outline of a tiger on top of the foreground.

6. Add patterns on the fur with orange, yellow and black.

7. Let the black stripes blend with the other colours where they overlap.

8. Draw lots of long grass in front of the tiger with greens and brown.

Colour and patterns

Oil pastels give you strong, vibrant colours. Use them to experiment with colours. Try putting different colours together and see how one colour affects another.

The blue square in the yellow square looks brighter than the same blue in the grey.

The green in the red square appears to be stronger than the same green in the grey square.

Experimenting with colours

Try putting different warm colours together.

Try cool colours, such as greens and blues.

Try warm and cool colours, in thick and thin stripes.

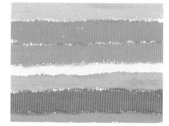

Experiment with bright and pale colours together.

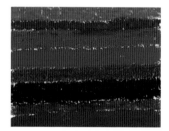

Try dark colours, such as blue, purple and brown.

Do alternate stripes of dark and light colours.

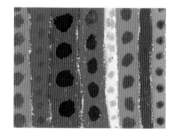

Draw spots along the stripes. Make them different sizes.

Draw thin lines or zigzags along some stripes.

A card idea

1. Draw a large box with a purple pastel. Draw an orange box inside.

2. Draw yellow triangles. Fill in between them with green.

3. Outline the triangles with a darker green. Add red dots.

4. Draw a red fence. Add a purple line down one side.

5. Draw the hen's body and colour it in. Leave a blank circle for the eye.

6. Add the beak, plumage, tail and feet. Fill them in and add stripes to the feet.

7. Fill in the sky. Add some shading with darker blue and purple around the edges.

8. Add some black lines to the hen's body. Outline the eye and add a pupil.

Oil pastel effects

ANY WHITE PAPER

Stained glass effect

Draw the outline in pencil first if you want to.

Press hard.

1. Fold your paper in half, then open it out. Draw half a butterfly with a black oil pastel.

2. Fold the paper in half again, then rub all over one side with the handle of a pair of scissors.

3. Unfold the paper. Use the pastel to draw over the faint outline of the other half of the butterfly.

4. Draw leaves in the background. Paint inks in the sections between all the outlines.

Ink outlines

Leave a gap between each section.

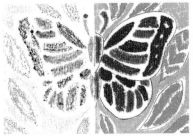

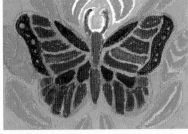

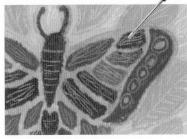

1. Follow steps 1-3 on page 74, but use a pencil to draw the outline. Fill in the spaces between the outline with oil pastels.

2. Paint all over your picture with a bright colour of ink. It will fill the gaps between the coloured sections.

3. Use the edge of a screwdriver to scratch details on the butterfly's wings and on the leaves in the background.

Wax crayons

Wax crayons can be used in lots of different ways. You can get lots of shades with one crayon by varying the amount of pressure you use. You can also mix them to make different colours. They are also good for doing rubbings and resist effects.

This shows some different shades you can get when you vary the pressure as you draw.

You can also mix wax crayons, although they don't blend together as well as chalk or oil pastels.

Wax resist stars

Press hard.

1. Draw stars all over your paper. Use two colours for each star. Add a trail from each star.

2. Mix up lots of dark blue watercolour paint in a pot. Don't make it too thin and watery.

3. Brush the paint across the paper, covering your drawing. The crayon resists the paint.

Fantasy bird

1. Draw a large bird with a pencil. Press lightly to get a faint outline.

Look at the big picture to see the white lines to draw.

2. Draw feathers on the head, body and tail with a white wax crayon. Draw lines on the feet, too.

3. Mix up some orange paint in a pot. Paint all over the picture.

4. Use a fine brush to paint details on the body and head Use dark red paint.

5. Add more details to the feathers using the dark red paint.

6. Paint around the eye, beak and feet. Add stripes to them.

Wax resist rubbings
THIN WHITE PAPER

1. Snap a wax crayon in half. Then, peel off any protective paper around it.

2. Lay a piece of thin paper on a textured surface, such as corrugated cardboard.

3. Rub the side of the crayon over the paper so that a pattern of the texture appears.

4. Paint over your rubbing with a contrasting colour of watercolour paint or ink.

5. Do more rubbings on different surfaces. Paint the rubbings in different colours.

6. On another piece of paper, draw a street of houses. Make each one different.

7. Cut the rubbings into strips. Glue on three or four pieces to make one house.

8. Add windows, doors, roof tiles and brickwork on top with a black wax crayon.

More resist effects

ANY THICK PAPER

1. Using bright wax crayons, draw a patterned stripe near the bottom of the paper.

2. Use different crayons to draw buildings. Add lots of domes, towers and windows.

3. Add some trees. Use bright crayons to colour in the walls and roofs of the buildings.

4. Paint all over the picture with a dark shade of ready-mix or poster paint.

5. Dab a damp, crumpled cloth over the waxy parts to lift off some of the paint.

6. Leave it to dry. Then, scratch patterns and shading into the crayon with a fingernail.

Cracked wax effect

THIN PAPER, SUCH AS TYPING PAPER

This is a different resist technique using wax crayons. It works best if your picture covers the paper.

Cracks appear in the crayoned parts when you screw up the paper (see step 3). These allow the paint to seep through, leaving a cracked effect.

1. Draw a flower in a pot with wax crayons. Colour them in, pressing hard.

2. Fill in the background with crayon. Press hard and leave no gaps.

3. Crumple the paper in from the corners. Be careful not to tear it.

4. Open out the paper. Crumple it again, so that you get lots of cracks.

5. Flatten your picture. Paint all over with dark poster paint or ready-mix.

6. Make sure that you have brushed paint into all the cracks.

7. Rinse both sides under a tap. Let the water drip off. Leave it to dry.

Use a warm setting on your iron.

8. If your picture is crinkly, iron it between two pieces of newspaper.

Creating textured papers

Many of the pages in this book have coloured backgrounds. These pages tell you how some of them were created and also gives you other ideas. Also look on pages 126-127 and 212-215 for more techniques.

This paper was created by dropping blobs of ink onto wet watercolour paper.

This rubbing was done with yellow wax crayon on the large holes of a cheese grater. The rubbing was then painted with ink.

This rubbing was done on the small holes on a cheese grater. See pages 78-79 for more rubbings.

For this effect, sprinkle salt onto wet watercolour paint. Let it dry, then rub off all the salt. See page 58 for a picture using this technique.

Paint a piece of plastic foodwrap with paint. Lay a piece of paper on top. Rub lightly over the paper, then lift it off (see pages 24 and 26).

This background was also done with paint on plastic foodwrap (see below left).

These pieces were painted with a household paintbrush. Paint on one colour, then brush another colour on top when dry. See pages 90-91 for a background like this.

This paper was painted with watercolour paints. It was then spattered with clean water while the paint was wet. Step 6 on page 31 shows you how to spatter.

Rub the side of a wax crayon over a piece of paper then paint it all over (see the background on page 80).

Spattered paper collage

COLOURED PAPER, SUCH AS SUGAR PAPER OR POSTER PAPER

Weight the newspaper with small stones.

1. This can be quite messy so do this outdoors. Put your paper onto some newspapers.

2. Put some ready-mix paint into a container. Add water to make it runny.

3. Dip an old toothbrush into the paint. Then, hold the brush over the paper.

4. Pull a ruler along the brush towards you, so the paint spatters onto the paper.

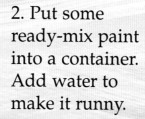

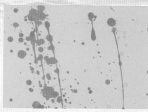

5. Keep spattering more paint on top until you get the effect you want. Let it dry.

6. Mix another colour of paint and spatter it in the same way on top of the first one.

7. To get big spatters, dip a household paintbrush into runny paint.

8. Flick the brush sharply downwards over the paper. Repeat with more paint.

9. Carry on flicking the paint until you have the pattern you want. Leave it to dry.

10. Draw the outline of a frog and leaves on the back of the big spattered paper.

11. Draw some bullrushes and a strip for water on the finely spattered paper.

12. Cut out the shapes and glue them onto a piece of contrasting paper.

Tissue paper painting

ANY THICK PAPER

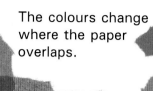

The colours change where the paper overlaps.

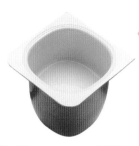

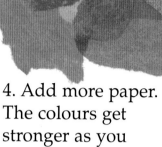

1. Rip some shapes from different colours of tissue paper.

2. Put some PVA glue into a pot. Mix in a few drops of water.

3. Glue the tissue shapes onto white paper. Overlap some pieces.

4. Add more paper. The colours get stronger as you build up the layers.

Draw on top of the tissue paper. You don't need to outline the paper exactly.

Add dots and lines to the leaves.

Poppies

1. Tear red and orange tissue paper into large petal shapes.

2. Glue one petal. Press it on to a large piece of white paper.

3. Add three more petals. Overlap and crumple the paper in places.

4. Cut leaves and stems from tissue paper. Glue them around the poppies.

5. Brush glue over the poppies. This makes them slightly shiny.

6. When the glue is completely dry, use a thin felt-tip to add details.

Making cards and frames

1. Fold some thin cardboard in half. Run a fingernail along the fold several times.

2. Lay your picture on the folded cardboard. Mark the corners with a pencil.

3. Lay the picture on newspaper. Glue the back of it, from the middle out to the edges.

4. Position the picture on the card, matching the pencil marks you made.

This small watercolour painting was mounted on coloured paper before being glued on.

 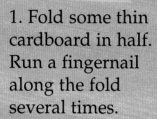 

5. Place a clean sheet of paper over the picture and press it evenly all over.

6. Put the card under some books overnight. This ensures that the picture is flat.

The details on this card were added with a gold felt-tip pen.

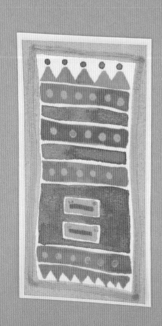

This card was decorated with tissue paper shapes.

Frames

Use a craft knife.

1. Cut a shape, bigger than your picture from thickish cardboard.

2. Cut another piece of cardboard, the same size for a backing.

3. Lay the picture on the first piece of cardboard. Use a pencil to draw around it.

4. Draw lines 5mm inside the pencil line. Then, cut around the inside shape.

5. Tape the picture onto the frame. Glue the backing and press the frame onto it.

Decorate your frame before you tape the picture to it.

The frame above has little pieces of ripped tissue paper glued on.

More ideas

On these pages and the next two pages, you will find lots more ideas which use techniques explained earlier in this part of the book.

The technique of blowing ink through a straw was used for these fish (see pages 54-55).

The picture above has pieces of spattered paper glued together to make a collage (see pages 86-87).

The flowers and butterflies below, and hedgehog on page 93, have all been painted using different shades of ink (see page 42-43).

These dolphins were cut from tissue paper, then strips of tissue paper were glued on for waves (see pages 88-89).

The pictures above were done with tissue paper and acrylic paint (see pages 12-13).

The red and orange pattern on the right was painted with acrylic paints. The dots were added with a cotton bud (see pages 14-15).

This lion was done by blowing ink and then painting on top (see pages 54-55).

These flowers were masked out. Paint was sponged around the shapes instead of spattered (see pages 30-31).

These flowers and leaves are ripped from tissue paper then glued onto paper (see pages 88-89).

To get a grainy effect like the one in the jungle scene and the two pictures below, sprinkle salt onto wet watercolour paint (see pages 58-59).

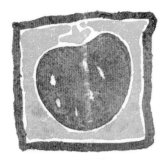

This turtle is a collage of patterns scratched into thick acrylic paint (see pages 10-11).

This tree is an elastic band print (see pages 24-25).

This snail is another idea for using ripped tissue paper (see pages 88-89).

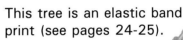

Index